OUR SOLAR SYSTEM

Space Walks

BY DANA MEACHEN RAU

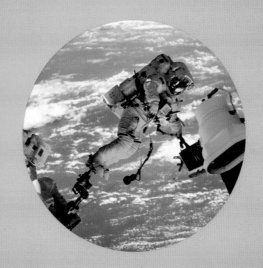

Content Adviser: Dr. Stanley P. Jones, Assistant Director, Washington, D.C., Operations, NASA-Sponsored Classroom of the Future

Science Adviser: Terrence E. Young Jr., M.Ed., M.L.S., Jefferson Parish (Louisiana) Public School System

Reading Adviser: Susan Kesselring, M.A., Literacy Educator, Rosemount-Apple Valley-Eagan (Minnesota) School District

COMPASS POINT BOOKS

MINNEAPOLIS, MINNESOTA

For Charlie and Allison—D.M.R

Compass Point Books
3109 West 50th Street, #115
Minneapolis, MN 55410

Visit Compass Point Books on the Internet at *www.compasspointbooks.com*
or e-mail your request to *custserv@compasspointbooks.com*

Photographs ©: NASA, cover, 1, 4, 6, 7 (all), 8, 9, 10 (all), 11, 12, 13, 14, 15, 17, 18–19, 20, 21, 22, 23 (all), 25, 26, 27, 28–29; MPI/Getty Images, 3, 5; DigitalVision, 27 (inset).

Editor: Nadia Higgins
Lead Designer/Page production: The Design Lab
Photo researcher: Svetlana Zhurkina
Educational Consultant: Diane Smolinski

Managing Editor: Catherine Neitge
Art Director: Keith Griffin
Production Director: Keith McCormick
Creative Director: Terri Foley

Library of Congress Cataloging-in-Publication Data
Rau, Dana Meachen, 1971–
 Space walks / by Dana Meachen Rau : Nadia Higgins, editor.
    p. cm. — (Our solar system)
 Includes index.
 ISBN 0-7565-0851-7 (hardcover)
 1. Extravehicular activity (Manned space flight)—Juvenile literature. I. Higgins, Nadia. II. Title.
 TL1096.R38 2005
 629.45'84—dc22   2004015569

Table of Contents

A New Way to Explore

☆ In 1965, astronaut Edward White II (1930–1967) was one of the first people to see space as few had before. He was not looking through a telescope from Earth. He was not looking through a window in his spacecraft. He was exploring space in a new way. He took a walk in outer space.

On June 3, 1965, Edward White became ▶ the first American to go on a space walk.

In 1969, astronauts Neil Armstrong (1930–) and Edwin "Buzz" Aldrin (1930–) performed another type of space walk—a moon walk. They landed their spacecraft on the moon and walked around on its slippery, dusty surface. There was some gravity on the moon. Bouncing got them around much faster than walking in their stiff space suits.

Gravity is the force that pulls people down to the ground. In space, there is no feeling of gravity. On his space walk, White felt as if he weighed nothing. So he was not really walking. He was floating. Safe inside his space suit, White looked like he was swimming in the black air.

A space walk is also called an EVA, which stands for extravehicular activity. Astronauts perform EVAs from space stations, where they live in space for months at a time. They have also space walked during space shuttle missions. The men and women who perform EVAs are not just space walkers. They are space workers with important jobs to do.

Astronaut Daniel M. Tani performs ▼
an EVA in 2001.

Space Working

✦ Today, EVA astronauts are like construction workers. They are helping to build the International Space Station, which is a huge spacecraft where astronauts from all over the world will live and work. The station is expected to be finished in 2010 and will probably take about 1,900 hours of space walks to complete. Workers will be connecting large pieces of the station, as well as small power lines between all of its parts.

▲ *Astronauts work on the International Space Station.*

◀ *Astronaut Lee M. E. Morin carries a small piece of the International Space Station.*

In the 1980s and 1990s, an important job of astronauts in space was to work with satellites. There are hundreds of satellites in orbit around Earth. These machines gather information from Earth and then send the information back to Earth again. Weather satellites look at storms and clouds. Some satellites take pictures of the land to help us make maps. Other satellites are used for communication. Without satellites, you would not be able to watch some of your favorite television shows or call a friend on your telephone.

The robotic arm of a space shuttle ▼ grabs a satellite in outer space.

A satellite sends messages all over Earth. On the ground, a large satellite dish sends signals up into the sky. The satellite takes in the signals and sends them down to another dish on another part of the globe. Signals can be sent from countries far away from each other.

Many satellites that are up in space now were launched with the help of space walkers. A satellite was loaded into a space shuttle on Earth. The shuttle brought it into space, and the satellite was sent into orbit. When astronauts put a satellite into orbit, they needed to perform EVAs.

Sometimes they needed to repair a satellite that was already out in space. A long, robotic arm attached to the shuttle grabbed the satellite. The arm brought the satellite into the shuttle's payload bay, which was open to space like

▲ *Astronaut Linda M. Godwin works near the robotic arm of the space shuttle* Endeavour.

a mechanic's garage. Then the astronauts fixed the satellite in the open payload bay. They might have patched a hole, replaced a part, or tightened a bolt.

Two astronauts wait for the right opportunity to grab a satellite. They will bring the satellite into their space shuttle's payload bay. ▷

The payload bay of a space shuttle ▽

In 1993, a team of astronauts was sent on a very important repair mission. They went to fix the Hubble Space Telescope, a special telescope that had been sent into space in 1990. Hubble can take photos of areas of space we cannot see from Earth. After its launch, the telescope started sending back fuzzy pictures. The astronauts fixed Hubble in space, replacing many parts and adding new ones.

◄ *Two astronauts work on replacing a part of the Hubble Space Telescope.*

Training for Space

★ How does an astronaut practice for working in space where it feels like there is no gravity? There is no place on Earth where gravity is not pulling us down. Being underwater is the closest we can get to experiencing the feeling of space walking.

Astronauts practice space walking at a giant pool near the Johnson Space Center in Houston, Texas. It is the largest indoor pool in the world—about as long as

Astronaut Janet L. Kavandi stands on ▸ the platform that will lower her into the training pool.

five-and-a-half school buses and about three times deeper than a usual swimming pool's deepest end.

A huge life-size model of the International Space Station lies at the bottom of the pool. The astronauts practice over and over again the jobs they will have to do. At first, the astronauts wear scuba suits with air tanks in the water. A team of scuba divers—at least four per astronaut—teaches the astronauts how to move around and work on the model. When

▲ *Astronauts rely on scuba divers to teach them how to move easily underwater.*

they are comfortable, the astronauts wear their space suits underwater. Each astronaut spends about 100 hours in the pool to train for an EVA.

Astronauts practice the jobs they will ▼ be doing later at the International Space Station.

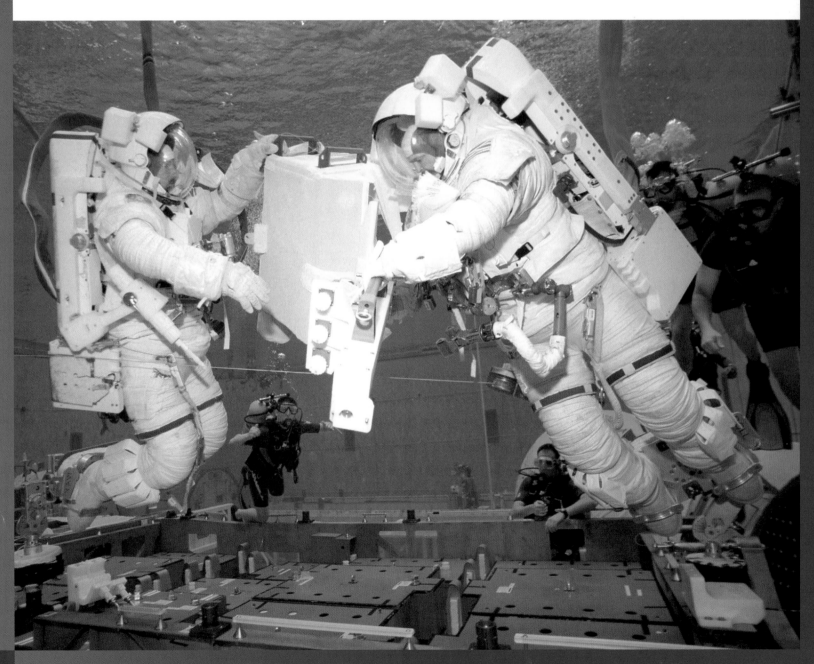

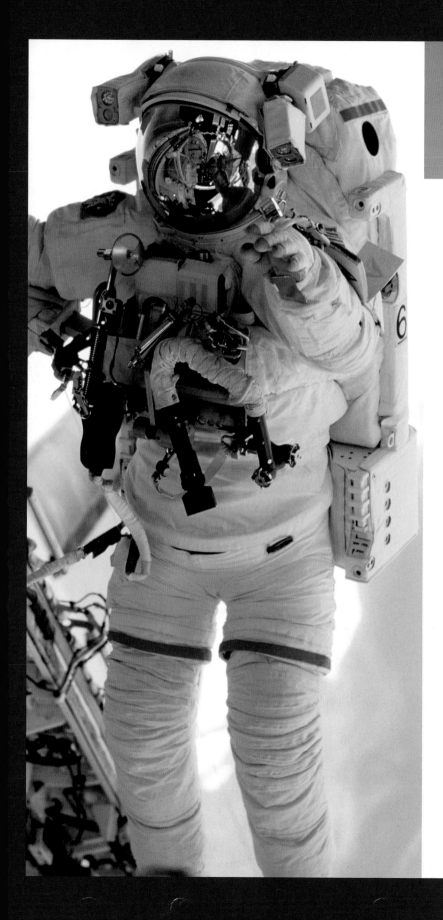

Protection in Space

✦ Inside a space shuttle or the International Space Station, the air is safe to breathe and the temperature is comfortable. Outside, however, space is a dangerous place. An astronaut needs to wear a space suit for protection. The suit is like a mini-spacecraft that holds the astronaut. It keeps the astronaut safe and comfortable so he or she can get work done.

There is no air in space. The space suit provides air for

◀ *A space suit makes space walks possible. It protects an astronaut from the extreme dangers of outer space.*

the astronaut to breathe. A special backpack contains enough oxygen to last an astronaut six to eight hours.

On Earth, air is also always pressing down on us. It's hard to think of air as weighing anything, but the air pressing down on you actually weighs a lot. This is called air pressure. You can't feel the weight of air, though, because it is pressing in on you from all sides. In space, there is no air pressure. Without pressure, your blood would fill with bubbles and your skin would blow up like a balloon. By the time you could count to 15, you would pass out. The space suit puts pressure on the astronaut so that his or her body stays healthy.

The temperature in space is another hazard. It can be very hot or very cold. When the sun is visible, temperatures can reach as high as 250° Fahrenheit (121° Celsius). When it is dark, temperatures drop down to about -250°F (-157°C). The space suit keeps the astronaut's temperature comfortable no matter how hot or cold it is outside.

An astronaut also needs protection from micrometeoroids, which are very tiny pieces of dust or rock flying through space. They may be tiny, but they are dangerous. Because they are so small, astronauts can't see them coming, so there is no way to avoid them. They zip through space at incredible speeds and could easily rip through an astronaut's skin. The suit's many layers protect the astronaut's skin from this flying dust.

▼ Astronaut Susan J. Helms poses with empty space suits aboard the International Space Station.

Some micrometeoroids travel up to 50 miles (80 kilometers) per second. That's about 3,000 times as fast as a car on the highway. Besides flying dust, the astronauts also have to look out for flying tools, screws, or other small pieces mistakenly left behind by previous space walkers.

The Parts of the Suit

⭐ A space suit covers every inch of an astronaut's body. The suit is made of fabric, metal, fiberglass, and plastic. It has so many pieces that it takes 15 minutes to put on. An astronaut puts on a space suit in the air lock. This is a room in the spacecraft where the suits are stored.

First, an astronaut puts on a special type of long underwear. It is covered with little tubes. Water flows through these tubes to keep the astronaut cool while

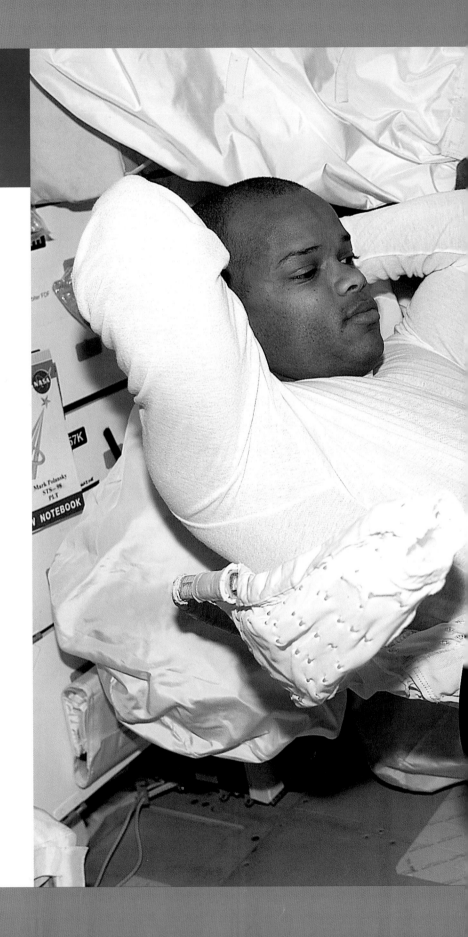

Astronaut Robert L. Curbeam slides ▶ into the bottom half of a space suit.

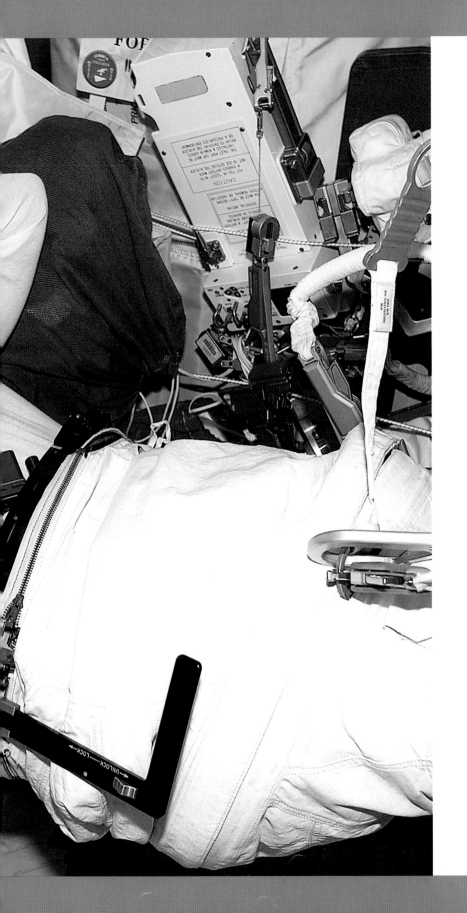

working. Next, the astronaut slides into the pants of the suit. Metal rings lock boots into place.

The part of the suit that covers the top half of the body goes on next. This part is stiff and mounted to the wall of the air lock. The astronaut floats and wriggles into the top of the suit. Another metal ring locks the top and bottom together.

A special computer is mounted onto the chest of the suit. It gives the astronaut information about the suit, such as the levels of oxygen and water. The astronaut cannot look down and read the display directly. Instead, a mirror attached to the wrist of the suit is used to read the front of the display.

Next, the astronaut pulls on a tight-fitting communications cap. Once the suit is completely on, the astronaut's ears will be covered by several layers of material. He or she won't be able to hear the other crew members. This cap has a radio that lets the astronauts talk to one another.

Astronaut Peggy A. Whitson floats ▶ near the top half of a suit, which is mounted on the wall of the air lock.

Finally, the gloves and helmet lock into place. The helmet has a sun visor, like sunglasses, to protect the astronaut from the sun's bright light. It also has lights on the sides for when the sun has set. Some helmets have a camera on the top to take pictures while the astronaut is working.

The suit also contains a drink bag and an energy snack bar near the astronaut's mouth. A simple turn of the head gets the astronaut a sip or bite.

When the suit is on, and the astronaut gets used to breathing the oxygen from the backpack, he or she is ready to leave the air lock. Now the space walk can begin.

▼ *Astronaut Michael J. Massimino waves to crew members inside a space shuttle.*

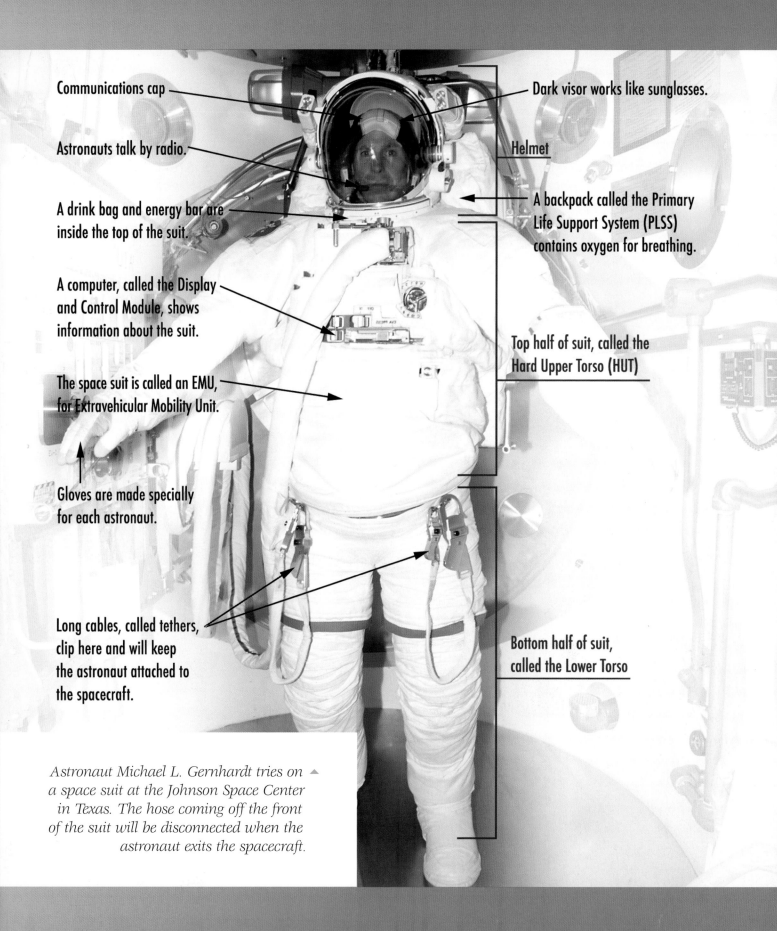

Communications cap

Astronauts talk by radio.

A drink bag and energy bar are inside the top of the suit.

A computer, called the Display and Control Module, shows information about the suit.

The space suit is called an EMU, for Extravehicular Mobility Unit.

Gloves are made specially for each astronaut.

Long cables, called tethers, clip here and will keep the astronaut attached to the spacecraft.

Dark visor works like sunglasses.

Helmet

A backpack called the Primary Life Support System (PLSS) contains oxygen for breathing.

Top half of suit, called the Hard Upper Torso (HUT)

Bottom half of suit, called the Lower Torso

Astronaut Michael L. Gernhardt tries on a space suit at the Johnson Space Center in Texas. The hose coming off the front of the suit will be disconnected when the astronaut exits the spacecraft.

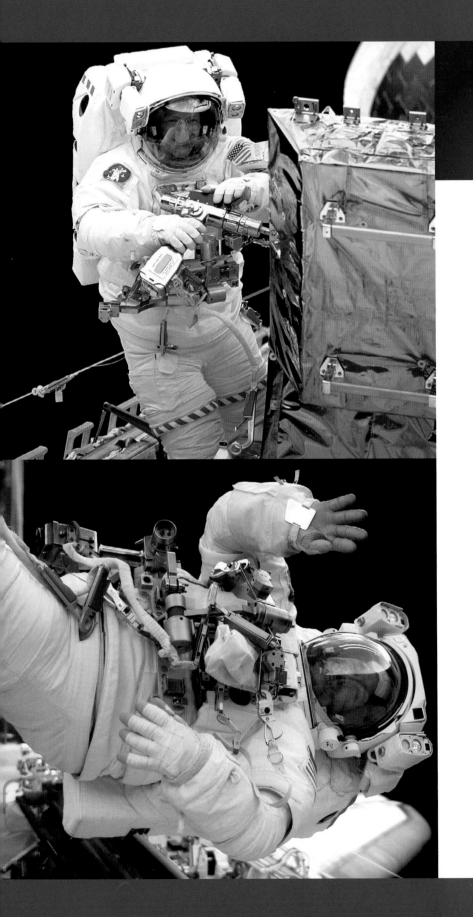

Moving Around Out There

✨ The suit protects the astronaut in space, but it is very hard to move around in one. The suit is like a big balloon. Bending is very difficult. So the suit is made with many joints in the same places you have joints in your body, such as your shoulders, wrists, and waist. The gloves have many joints as well so that an astronaut's fingers can bend and use the tools correctly.

▲ Astronaut Claude Nicollier uses a power tool.

◄ An astronaut's tools connect to the space suit so they won't float away.

The tools used in space are like the wrenches and hammers you might have in a toolbox on Earth, only their handles are much bigger. This makes them easier to use with the bulky gloves. The tools also connect to the space suit in some way. Some connect by hooks. Otherwise, if an astronaut dropped a tool, it would float away!

Astronauts have to make sure they don't float away, too. There is nothing to grab onto to stop them from drifting off into space. There is nothing for them to push against either, such as the ground or water. So even if they move their legs as if to walk, or pump their arms like swimmers, they will still stay in one place. For this reason, astronauts are always attached to the spacecraft with tethers.

A tether is a strong cord that works like a leash. One end is clipped onto the astronaut and the other end to a ring or rail on the spacecraft. The astronaut pulls on the tether to swing around and move from place to place.

On the International Space Station, astronauts use tethers, and they also hold on to handholds and footholds placed all over the outside of the station. They move like rock climbers to get where they need to go.

▼ *An astronaut at the International Space Station uses both tethers and footholds to get around.*

tether

foothold

In case the tether breaks, an astronaut wears a special safety device that fits onto the back of the space suit. If an astronaut ever floats away from the shuttle or space station, this device works like a life jacket. Jets of gas shoot out that push the astronaut back to the spacecraft and back to safety.

The safety device on the back of a space suit is called a SAFER, which stands for Simplified Aid for EVA Rescue. No astronaut has ever had to use a SAFER.

SAFER

MARS →

Space Walks and Beyond

✦ Spacewalking has become one of the most important parts of exploring space. The astronauts' hard work prepares us for even more exciting adventures. The satellites they launch and repair open up new ways to see our own world as well as outer space. The International Space Station they are building is paving the way for long stays in space, perhaps even trips to Mars. "Mars walking"

◄ *The National Aeronautics and Space Administration (NASA) asked an artist to make this illustration showing what space exploration to Mars might look like.*

could be the next step for astronauts, and new space suits will need to be designed.

On the next clear and starry night, go out for a walk. When you look up at the sky, think about what you can see. Then think about the astronauts in space. On a space walk, they are working hard, but they often stop to enjoy the sky, too. They see the beautiful ball of Earth from a view only a few people can enjoy.

More than 220 miles (352 kilometers) ▸
above Earth, astronaut David A. Wolf
enjoys a spectacular view of the planet.

Glossary

air lock—a special room on a spacecraft with a door to the outside; also where the space suits are stored

fabric—cloth

fiberglass—a strong material made from thin strands of glass that is used in space suits

joints—places on a space suit or on the body that easily bend

micrometeoroids—tiny pieces of rock or dust shooting so quickly through space that they could harm a space walker

oxygen—the gas humans and animals need to breathe to stay alive

payload bay—a large area in a space shuttle that holds cargo and opens to the outside

robotic—run by machines and computers

space shuttle—a planelike spacecraft that makes trips into space and lands again on Earth

telescope—a tool used by astronomers to collect information about distant objects; many important telescopes are not on Earth, but in outer space

tether—a cord that attaches a space walker to a spacecraft

Did You Know?

- The first person to walk in space was a Russian named Alexei Leonov (1934–). His spacecraft, *Voskhod 2,* brought him into space for his 12-minute walk in March 1965. The American Edward White walked in space a few months later.

- The first woman to walk in space was the American Kathryn D. Sullivan (1951–) in 1984.

- Do you wear extra layers on a cold day when you play outside? Imagine a suit with 14 layers. That is the thickness of the suit that astronauts on space shuttles use.

- One space suit costs about $12 million.

- Astronauts not only eat and drink in their space suits, but they can go to the bathroom in them, too. A special diaper called a maximum absorption garment collects their waste and is then thrown away.

- International Space Station suits are designed to be worn about 25 times until they need to be checked out and fixed back on Earth.

- To move around in space, Edward White used a small gun, called a Hand-Held Maneuvering Unit. It shot out bursts of gas that pushed him along in space.

Want to Know More?

AT THE LIBRARY

Editors of *YES Mag. The Amazing International Space Station.* Toronto: Kids Can Press, 2003.

Gifford, Clive. *The Kingfisher Facts and Records Book of Space.* New York: Kingfisher, 2001.

Pascoe, Elaine. *International Space Station.* San Diego: Blackbirch Press, 2003.

Spangenburg, Ray, and Kit Moser. *The History of NASA.* New York: Franklin Watts, 2000.

ON THE WEB

For more information on **space walks,** use FactHound to track down Web sites related to this book.

1. Go to www.facthound.com
2. Type in a search word related to this book or this book ID: **0756508517**.
3. Click on the *Fetch It* button.

Your trusty FactHound will fetch the best Web sites for you!

ON THE ROAD

National Air and Space Museum
Sixth and Independence Avenue Southwest
Washington, DC 20560
202/357-2700
To learn more about the solar system and space exploration

The Kansas Cosmosphere and Space Center
1100 N. Plum
Hutchinson, KS 67501
800/397-0330
To see a large collection of spacecraft and a detailed history of space flight through time

Kennedy Space Center
Visitor Complex
Kennedy Space Center, FL 32899
321/452-2121
To see exhibits on the history of space flight and even catch a shuttle launch

NASA Goddard Space Flight Center
Visitor Center
Greenbelt, MD 20771
301/286-9041
To see exhibits of NASA's many space missions

Index

◄ **About the Author:** *Dana Meachen Rau loves to study space. Her office walls are covered with pictures of planets, astronauts, and spacecraft. She also likes to look up at the sky with her telescope and write poems about what she sees. Ms. Rau is the author of more than 100 books for children, including nonfiction, biographies, storybooks, and early readers. She lives in Burlington, Connecticut, with her husband, Chris, and children, Charlie and Allison.*